The Little Book

D0767060

Do

About Women

Zymurgy Publishing, 2006

The moral rights of authors Amanda Thomas and Martin Ellis have been asserted.

All rights reserved. No part of this publication may be reproduced, stored in a retrieval system, or transmitted in any form or by any means without the prior written permission of Zymurgy Publishing. Whilst every effort has been made to ensure the accuracy of the facts contained in this publication, no responsibility can be accepted by the author or Zymurgy Publishing for errors or omissions or their consequences.

A CIP catalogue record for this book is available from the British library.
Cover design Nick Ridley
Printed in Malta on behalf of Latitude Press Limited

ISBN 978 1903506 22 6

Published by Zymurgy Publishing,
Newcastle upon Tyne
1 0 9 8 7 6 5 4 3
© Zymurgy Publishing 2006
reprinted 2010
Many thanks to the following people for their suggestions: Paul Chadwick, Mark Farrer, Leon Gingell, Steve Ingham, Andrew Smith, Sheila Spencer, Dorothy Thomas and Dave Wheatstone

"Women and cats will do as they please, men and dogs should relax and get used to the idea."

Robert A. Heinlein

Women claim to have a sexual appetite. Why do many appear to be on a strict diet?

Women seem to put more energy into (and derive greater pleasure from) analysing and discussing sex than actually doing it – what's that about?

Women have a sexual appetite just as great as men (and sometimes greater).

If men wonder why their partner behaves like she's on a sexual crash diet and would prefer her to be binge eating, they should get a grip and ask themselves a few questions.

Why are women's magazines full of sex?

Flick through women's magazines and they appear to be obsessed with sex, the subject creeps into nearly every feature.

Women's mags like to take a more narrative approach as opposed to men's mags which have all the goods in the shop window. Women like to be reassured that they're doing it right and that others have the same problems. Indeed it's great to discover that compared to some people you've got nothing to worry about.

Why do women read so many romantic novels?

Romantic novels are formulaic and predictable – the characters could surely only exist in a book. Mills and Boon, bodice-rippers, shopping and shagging, Aga sagas and the rest, they are as close a representation to life as science fiction.

Whatever the time or the genre women like to read about romance particularly if they're not getting any. Never mind boddice-rippers, today's women are more concerned with how to remain sexy and seductive whilst trying to get their *Magic Knickers* off in a hurry on a date that's going better than anticipated.

Why do women share intimate secrets with friends?

Women confide and discuss the physical side of their relationships with each other. Men never drone on to their mates about their acts of intimacy.

A problem shared is a problem doubled.

Surely it's good to talk and gather sex tips? The use of 'drone' here indicates that men view sex as irksome and are far happier discussing the ins and outs of the offside rule.

Why are women more into analysing relationships than men?

Women seem to know the state of everyone's relationships - who has just started seeing each other, who has just split up, who is setting up home together and so on and so on.

Talking about the state of the union with one's girlfriends is a much more alluring topic than just talking about make-up, clothes and work all the time.

Why do women insist on trying to mould their bloke into their ideal guy?

Why can't women be happy with a bloke the way they found him?

Very rarely do you find an item of clothing 'off the peg' that's a perfect fit. The same applies to blokes – you take the nearest thing to it and customise it.

"Whatever women must do they must do twice as well as men to be thought half as good. Luckily, this is not difficult."

Charlotte Whitton

Why isn't there a male equivalent of misogyny?

So there is a word to describe men who hate women, fair enough. Whilst it is difficult to understand why a man would hate women, it is not surprising that the rich English language has a word for this sad attitude. There are women who hate men, why is there no word to describe them?

There is a word actually, seeing as the question has been raised - misandry. If men were more articulate they would know this word already.

Why do women use feminine arousal sprays?

Surely men are more than capable of stimulating their partners in the right places without having to resort to artificial means?

Feminine arousal products (sprays, oils and creams) enhance sexual pleasure by hitting the spot (e.g. the clitoris) without deviation or hesitation. They are now fully mainstream as they can be found on the shelves of pharmacies. And anything with a warning that it "may contain nuts" demands further investigation. [Always read the label - he he].

Why do men and women pack differently?

Women take up to a week when it takes men less than half an hour. Men throw some pants into a rucksack or holdall for a trip away plus a couple of T-shirts and their toothbrush. Women take enough clothes for a week (even if they're just away for the weekend), half their dressing table contents and who knows what from the bathroom. Why?

Oh yes - the old 'taking everything but the kitchen sink' routine. It's not like this for everyone but the female quality of being able to think ahead along with the legacy of Brownies means that every major scenario is considered every time a woman leaves home. So her handbag or luggage contains an arsenal of equipment to cope with most eventualities.

Why do women tidy and clean the house before going away on holiday?

There are two reasons for this. The first reason is that enough chaos will be created on return from holiday without having to worry about the housework 'n' all. It's depressing enough on its own without adding post-holiday blues. The second reason is if you are visited by burglars whilst on holiday you don't want them to think you're scuzzy.

Why do women know the difference between dust and fluff?

If men did more hoovering this would be transparent.

Why do women with cleaners clean before they arrive?

It's not cleaning before the cleaner arrives - it's tidying up to make their job easier. Plus, if they are getting paid by the hour it maximises efficiency if they don't have to shift things around first. Isn't it obvious?

Why do women jabber on about work?

Women come home from work and believe that everyone is interested in a detailed description of their working day.

Women need to 'jabber on' about work because they're looking for empathy and evidence that they are not alone in the situations they experience 9-5. It was John Donne who said that "no man is an island" and he included women in that reckoning.

Why do women natter about nothing on the telephone to their best friends while their partner is trying to watch the telly, particularly during key football matches?

How are women supposed to know which matches are key and which ones aren't?

The goss on who's shagging who, where the best shoe sales are and the latest diet tips are all far more important.

Why do women iron in front of the telly when their partner is trying to watch it?

Multitasking is what women do and men wish they could. Watching the telly makes the boredom of ironing almost bearable. If men wish to swap, women would be delighted with a restricted view of *Coronation Street*.

Why do women warm their shivering cold feet on men?

While men are getting cosy in bed women are finishing the washing up so the least men can do is offer their bare backside up as a small token of gratitude. Really, household chores or not, women only do this because they can.

Why do women love shopping?

Why do women spend most of their free time shopping or reading magazines for ideas about what to buy when they're out shopping?

This is a gross overstatement. Some women love shopping, others view it as a chore similar to cleaning out the fridge. Men are best advised not to shop with women if they don't want to. Hordes of men hanging around department store changing rooms of a Saturday afternoon smacks of desperation.

Why do women buy stuff in the sales they'll never wear?

"A bargain is something you can't use at a price you can't resist."

Franklin Jones

Why do women take so long over the weekly shop?

It is important to consider our purchases, plan meals, check the labels for: gluten, wheat, carbs, sodium - you name it. Women shop with a purpose you see; while men shop with a spear and come back with beer, the paper and special offer Bakewell tarts.

Why do women buy loads of magazines?

Women don't seem to be able to pass a newsagents without buying a magazine, there seem to be more and more of them on the shelves all the time.

Women spend millions every year on magazines advising them how to spend their money. Apart from the sex tips magazines are full of gorgeous women and ideal homes. This is (like it or not) designed to be aspirational and it's something to work towards.

Why do women prioritise features like the colour when buying a car?

Men are practical about purchases whereas women are sensual. The priorities for men when buying a car are performance, functionality, 0-60 speed and a CD/MP3 player and for women it's colour, reliability, miles per gallon and the provision of a cup holder.

Do women look at the male underwear section in catalogues?

Yes women do but not to perv over the men's bodies or to see who's got the best undercarriage. We do this for a laugh while researching Christmas presents for our notoriously difficult to buy for fathers.

Why according to research do over 70% of women wear the wrong size bra?

Hormones, time and bread do unnecessary things to women. Perfectly fitting underwear in the morning can be agony by the afternoon so leave it! Bra-fitting services are taken by most women during their lifetime but suffering the indignity of having your boobs wrenched around by a department store tape measure-wearing matron (AKA a corsetiere) with cold hands and a warm smile is an experience rarely repeated.

Why do women buy sparkly blouses that are not machine washable?

Sequins, glittery patterns, delicate embroidery and sensitive fabrics all require careful hand washing. Totally impractical, surely it would be wise to buy clothes that are easy to wash?

When there's a gorgeous piece of clothing begging to be taken home, worn and loved THIS is unavoidable. Who wants to be boring and practical all the time? Anyway, 'blouses' are what Miss Marple wears.

Why do women regularly insist on buying new colour co-ordinated lingerie?

Women regularly claim to have no matching bra and knicker sets, when their drawers are stuffed full of matching chewing-gum grey underwear.

Chewing-gum grey will never be 'the new black' so what women refer to as 'matching' is what they like to wear for best. This is not the garb worn only for church on a Sunday but when there's a chance that a bloke might see it. The old and tatty stuff is kept back for watching the telly in or wearing to the gym.

What does 'the new black' mean?

Women are always making references (verbally, in newspapers and magazines, or on telly) to 'the new black' but never white, blue, red etc.

Black clothing is very versatile as many women find it slimming, goes with everything in her wardrobe and thus is easy to wear. So when a new colour emerges with these same properties it is announced as 'the new black' as code for women to go out and buy some.

Why do women have 10 pairs of black shoes and sometimes 30-100 pairs overall?

They're not all the same. Women have shoes for best (heels), shopping (flats), work (sensible), pub (rock chick), for wearing with dresses (depending on the occasion), skirts (depending on the skirt) and trousers (depending on their length) plus the ones lost out the back of the wardrobe.

A recent survey conducted by *Harpers Bazaar* magazine found that 50% of women own more than 30 pairs of shoes and 8% own more than 100 pairs. While this seems indulgent it's worth noting that most women don't lead a *Harper's* life.

Why do women wear shoes they can't walk in?

It's incredibly frustrating, after a pleasant evening at the cinema, when you have to 'get a move on' to make last orders at the pub and you're with a woman hobbling along at a snail's pace.

This is because women like them, they make them feel sexy and they like a challenge – like men, cooking from scratch, hair removal and going shopping with no make-up on.

Why do women have handbags?

When women wear jeans or trousers why don't they put their money, keys and hankies in their pockets?

f women put stuff in their pockets it compromises a carefully chosen outfit - adding lumps.

Having a handbag avoids unnecessary spoiling of the lines, plus blokes always ask if they can put their stuff in there as well!

Why do women have driving shoes?

Driving shoes are an essential part of a woman's wardrobe. They are kept under the pedals of her car and are used to prolong the life of her proper shoes. This is boring, sensible yet necessary and if men ever attempted to drive in heels they would understand the apparent nonsense.

What are 'fat' clothes?

Some girls are bigger than others and some days even the smaller ones are bigger - this could be at a certain time of the month or after a long night on the town. So women have different clothes to hide or distract the eye from lumps, and these are called 'fat' or 'safe' clothes.

Why do women's clothes all come in set sizes, 8, 10, 12.........?

Surely it would make sense when buying clothes to know the waist size, inside leg, chest measurement, collar size and so on? Women are different shapes so if clothes were properly labelled, it would be easier to select garments that fit.

Male logic indeed. Perhaps it was Marks who started it, but could equally have been Spencer. Seriously, in the UK we're still holding on to the imperial system of sizing and measurements for clothes. Europe has long been metric but there still isn't a pan-European system. The BSI is making progress in this area so this question may be redundant soon.

Why can't women take a compliment?

Pay a woman a compliment and there is every chance that the reaction will be "what was wrong before?"

t's a given that men don't notice the same things that women notice. This makes women suspicious when they actually do notice. At best you may be homosexual and at worst you're having an affair. At these times it's best to put off any attempts at new ideas in the bedroom as the level of suspicion will be heightened.

Why do women's clothes button the 'other way' up?

Women's clothing is buttoned right over left, whilst men's clothing is buttoned left over right.

The convention dates from the time when ladies employed hand maidens to assist them and clothing was designed accordingly. Men have always dressed and undressed themselves.

Why do women have hairy fannies?

At school children are told about changes that take place during puberty but not usually told why.

While the purpose of pubic hair is not absolutely certain its main function is believed to assist the process of perspiration. Sweating helps to cool the body and disseminates pheromones which send out sexual signals.

Why do women have a greater pain threshold than men?

Women get a cold, toothache or injure themselves and they carry on – men think they're dying and go straight to bed.

It is believed that during the evolution of the species women have developed a higher pain threshold to cope with the physical demands of childbirth. This is partly because God intended to punish Eve (and therefore all women) for eating an apple. Speaking of pain, it is also worth noting here that periods are mandatory if you're female and so is playing hockey between the ages of 12-16.

Why aren't women as fascinated by breasts as much as men are?

It is commonly thought that male attraction to breasts links back to when men were babies and breasts were a source of food, comfort and security. As women were also breast-fed as babies why don't they share the same obsession?

Have breasts been unfairly annexed by women to assert power over men or to maintain a certain status? Nope! Whichever way women view their breasts it doesn't require them to be (like men and their 'bits') inspected, fiddled with or handled in any way every few minutes.

Why is it extremely rare for women to be colour-blind?

It may seem that far more men than women are colour-blind and this is absolutely true. The cause is genetic - for a man to be colour-blind the defective gene only needs to be passed on by one parent, for a female to be colour-blind both parents need to pass on the gene. Approximately 1 in 12 men and 1 in 200 women have colour vision defects (colour-blindness) according to The Institution of Engineering and Technology.

Biology

Why is it when you get loads of women living or working together they mysteriously all seem to have their period at the same time?

When women spend a fair amount of time together after a few months their menstrual cycles subconsciously become synchronised. Social signals are conveyed in the air between women by way of pheromones. Historically this had a practical application because nursing mothers who died could have their babies fed by another woman thereby ensuring the survival of the species.

Why do women do pelvic floor exercises?

Every breakfast TV fitness guru is always banging on about the pelvic floor – why?

The pelvic floor muscles hold the bladder and urethra (the tube that urine comes out of) in place. They are used when we urinate and relax at the same time as the bladder contracts (tightens) to let the urine out. These muscles get weaker as we get older, and also in women who've had children. So men and women should do pelvic floor exercises to avoid incontinence and to improve their sex lives. The exercises are also useful for men who have had prostate surgery.

Why are women, on average, shorter than men?

Throughout the world, across cultures and different ethnic backgrounds women tend to be shorter than men.

One explanation is that the bones that give height grow more slowly when puberty starts. As puberty starts earlier in females, it therefore follows that women will tend to be shorter than men. Another explanation is down to sexual selection – as humans evolved women favoured larger men as they were superior hunters.

Why do women have a moody before their period?

Women suffer from Premenstrual Syndrome (PMS) which will be explained to you when you get back from the Chinese – it's physiological, biological, non-denominational and – oh fuck off! Also illogical.

Why do women have a sweeter tooth than men?

Research suggests that the female hormone oestrogen may be at work here, explaining the increased preference for sweets among women rather than men. It's basic physiology dictating that women's bodies are saving up fat to support the growth of new life.

Why do women insist that they do not want any chips then help themselves to their partner's portion?

Women adamantly state that they do not want or wish to have chips, then tuck into their partner's portion with such efficiency that they nearly scoff the lot!

The female of the species is instinctively concerned about the health of themselves and those that are close to them. With health in mind, they decline chips for themselves and prevent their partner eating theirs. What's more if they are not your chips, they don't contain any calories.

Why do women obsess about food?

Women always seem to be on a diet: Atkins, F-Plan, Weight Watchers, GI and so on.

s it surprising that women are anxious about their figures when the fashion industry fills their magazines with tiny models and features about what they should and should not eat? Then there's the press coverage of which celebrities have gained weight, exposed their cellulite on holiday etc vying with the *100 Sexiest Women* polls favoured by the lads' mags.

Why do women like chocolate more than men?

According to *http://chocolate.org/* some 50% of women claim to prefer chocolate to sex.

Do you mean more women than men like chocolate? Chocolate cravings are admitted by 15% of men and around 40% of women. More than 300 different constituent compounds in chocolate have been identified, delivering all sorts of goodies in a 'psychoactive cocktail' of bliss. These include tryptophan (linked with enhanced serotonin function which typically diminishes anxiety), endorphins (reduces sensitivity to pain) and magnesium (which premenstrual women crave).

Why do women go to the hairdressers so often – surely it costs a fortune?

The longer hair is allowed to grow the more it becomes vulnerable to split ends and general poor condition. Women therefore schedule regular hair appointments to make their hair grow stronger and healthier. It's also a device to legitimately spend hours at the salon: reading their mags, drinking their tea and eyeing up their cute male trainees.

Why can't women throw properly?

When throwing a ball overarm, women raise their arm half way and flick the ball forward with a limp wrist action. The ball goes anywhere or nowhere.

Women aren't taught to throw properly from the start so all their technique is copied. They think cricket, with good intentions, and bottle out when it comes to the actual release because they're scared of throwing in the wrong direction or hurting someone (usually themselves).

Why do women run with pokey out arms flapping in all directions?

When women run for buses, play rounders, netball and other girly games their arms whirl around in an un-coordinated manner.

This is generally done to counterbalance the effect of wearing heels whilst running for a bus. Some women may not run in the most ergonomic manner but what about Kelly Holmes, Paula Radcliffe, Sally Gunnell and many other great sportswomen?

Why is it that many women can't reverse park?

Women only want to go forward in life and driving is just one example of this philosophy.

Does size matter?

Generations of women have reassured men that size does not matter, but in recent years some have enthused about very well-endowed men.

Knobs & Knockers - size matters but it's an individual thing. Not all women like big willies, simularly not all men like big boobs. More than a handful is a waste after all.

Why do women claim that every bathroom scale ever made is inaccurate?

Scales offer a different result on different surfaces. Bathroom, kitchen, hallway - every type of flooring influences the reading on a pair of scales. Women therefore are rarely satisfied with the result because they don't trust it.

"Women are like tea bags. We don't know our true strength until we are in hot water!"

Eleanor Roosevelt

What is feminism all about?

It was only ever about equality and it still is.

Why are women so cryptic?

Women suggest, imply and hint, then complain that men don't do as they are asked. What do they expect if they don't make themselves clearly understood?

It's like doing a crossword puzzle. The 'coffee time' one is easy and over too quickly. Challenge is a game for more than one player.

Why are women so impatient?

Women regularly whinge and complain, and whatever men do, it is never right.

When men get straight to the point there's no problem. Women are doers and therefore need to make rapid decisions on their behalf. Thankfully this is done with such efficiency that men are at the stage where they're still deciding which tie to wear.

Why do women shout and scream when they see male performers getting their kit off on a night out with the girls?

Women love to show their open appreciation of the male form and the artist(s) musical interpretation. It is the performance that women get a thrill from (long live the

Officer and a Gentleman routine) and increasing 'respect' is shown as more and more nudity is revealed.

Why do women have gay best friends?

It is common for women to be close friends with gay men, so why don't men have lesbian best friends?

Many men don't understand lesbians, anyway why would they want to hang around with you? A GBF (Gay Best Friend) is the only man that will be honest with a woman about her appearance, even if it causes upset. GBFs are also great to go furniture shopping with, they like cooking and they're impartial about giving relationship/ sex advice. A GBF is a man who is one of the girls.

Why can't you ask a woman her age?

When a woman is old enough to get into pubs and clubs without being asked her age all the fun slips out of it as it no longer represents a challenge and a chance to put two fingers up to the authorities. Thereafter, the only time a woman supplies her age is on her CV or a medical questionnaire. So please don't play the 'how old are you?' game unless Kofi Annan is in the room to mediate.

Why do women compliment each other on their appearance?

Whenever women meet up they go through a long rigmarole of commenting on each other's appearance. You don't get blokes exchanging compliments for ten minutes whenever they meet.

Women pay tribute to a good outfit/lipstick/hairdo because blokes are shit at it and if your mate is looking good she needs to know it. It's a genuine confidence booster unlike the images you see on tampon ads.

Why do women like to be given flowers?

Several studies have shown that receivers of flowers smile on contact. So the short answer is that flowers illicit positive feelings. Women feel closer to nature and delight at the affection when flowers are being proffered – even if they have been brought at the local petrol station.

Why can't women make their minds up?

That's absurd and also not true. No wait.....It's because women like to be flexible.

Why do women have parties selling all sorts of stuff from cosmetics and Tupperware to marital aids?

You wouldn't find blokes inviting their mates around to sell them things.

Where would we be without Tupperware? Can you ever have too much? These questions are best debated with girlfriends and wine at parties. Parties involving cosmetic are vehicles for pampering and what happens at *Ann Summers*' parties stays at *Ann Summers*' parties.

Why do women dress provocatively and then complain when they get male attention?

Women wind blokes up by wearing revealing clothes when they're out but snap your head off if you try and chat them up.

Men should learn that women dress for themselves and other women rather than men. It's great to be admired and flattered for a good choice of outfit but this is not a licence to stare at, talk to and/or touch a woman as it may be inappropriate.

Why do women have lengthy conversations on the phone with their mates when they're meeting them later that night?

If men did that we would run out of things to say within an hour. What's the point?

t's essential to know where the meeting will be, at what time and who with. 'Lengthy' conversations, by male and not female standards, are needed to ascertain the dress code for the event and the likely outlay in terms of cash. Also, an idea of the topics to be discussed is required so a woman can formulate her thoughts ahead of time.

Why do women who turn up at a social occasion wearing the same clothes make an issue out of it?

Men don't give a stuff when it happens to them. In fact, it can be a bonding experience when two men wearing the same shirt or jumper, for example, share the same taste in clothing "These are good, got mine in a sale........"

You're damned if you do and damned if you don't. If a woman has spent a lot of money on an outfit the expense is rendered void if someone else turns up wearing the same gear as her stab at individuality is lost.

Conversely, if she hasn't spent that much on her outfit the other woman will know exactly how cheap she is.

Social

Why do women have to speak to each other the day after they've been out on the town?

There needs to be a debriefing session after any gathering to ensure that everyone is clear on the issues discussed and to agree on any follow-up, if required.

What do women do with all the loo roll?

Women find uses for everyday objects far beyond what it actually says on the tin. Loo roll is used for wiping after the loo, for removing make-up, stemming the bloodshed of a shaving accident, mopping up toothpaste spills and stuffing into her bra to enhance her cleavage.

Why do women get so angry and upset about toilet seats being left up?

Surely it is far better to share a toilet seat with a bloke who lifts the seat up rather than pee on it?

This remains the one thing that universally divides men and women (except in developing countries where all you have is a hole in the ground). The issue is that women prefer not to handle a loo seat without rubber gloves on; and anyway the seat is more aesthetic when it is lowered.

Why do women spend an extra 15 minutes in the bathroom just as you're about to go out?

Women seem to be ready to go out (even putting their shoes and coat on) and then just as you make your way to the front door they disappear into the bathroom. Why is this?

Women do this because they want to have the opportunity of making last minute adjustments if required - they want their men to be proud to show them off in public. They also do this to subtly remind their men that they are in control of the relationship but mostly they do it just to piss them off.

Why do women spend so much time in the bathroom at home?

Women need to do essential maintenance in the bathroom – powdering their noses, for example. While they're in there they also check what other maintenance needs doing on the DIY front (it's good time management).

Why is there always a queue in the Ladies'?

Pub, club, gig, sports event or whatever; when it is busy women always have to queue for the Ladies.

Well, 'bunching' is caused around female public inconveniences (sic) for several reasons: the designers of such establishments are usually men, it involves more than just popping their urethra out and going to the lav is partly social.

Going to the pub/club loo is a great chance to have a gossip about what's going on in the world – i.e. who's shagging who.

ow do women know when to go to the Ladies' together?

Is it telepathy, osmosis or what?

If a woman needs to talk to her friend and her presence is required in the loo she will usually make a gesture to this end. This is mostly done with a combination of eye and neck movements that are undetectable by men.

TEN REASONS why women go to the Ladies' together

1   So that they can talk about men.

2   So that they can talk about women.

3   So they can wang on about their periods.

4   So that they can hold each other's hair out of the way if they're going to vomit.

5   It's handy to have a friend to share lipstick and eyebrow pencil with.

6   So they can play 'spot the loo roll' on each other's shoes.

7   To insure against the embarrassment of having their skirt tucked into their knickers.

8   When there's no loo roll (a common problem in urban areas) women can pass some to each other under the door.

9 When busy it sometimes helps to share a cubicle with a mate to ease congestion.

10   There's strength in numbers and if there's a crowd it's easier to wade through the throng with another.

"Why can't a woman be more like a man?"

Professor Higgins in

My Fair Lady